WINGS OF THE WHITE CRANE

WINGS OF THE WHITE CRANE

Poems of Tshangs dbyangs rgya mtsho
(1683-1706)

Translated by
G. W. HOUSTON

Historical Introduction by
HELMUT HOFFMANN

MOTILAL BANARSIDASS
Delhi :: Varanasi :: Patna

First Published in 1982
by MOTILAL BANARSIDASS
Indological Publishers and Booksellers
Head Office : Bungalow Road, Jawahar Nagar, Delhi-7
Branches : 1. *Chowk, Varanasi* 1 *(U. P.)*
2. *Ashok Rajpath, Patna-*4 *(Bihar*

Printed in India by
Shri Shantilal Jain, at Shri Jainendra Press,
*A-*45, *Phase-I, Industrial Area, Naraina, New Delhi-*28.
Published for Motilal Banarsidass by Narendra Prakash Jain

FOR JOYCE

she teaches me about love
and about myself—what a
long search it has been.

PREFACE

The reason for the title of this book is obvious to those who have studied Tibetan culture. The Sixth Dalai Lama promised his love that he would only go to Lithang and return. And, he prayed, if that be the word, for the wings of the white crane. Instead, he never returned. Whether he was killed by his captors who did not like his religion, or whether he escaped to live with his love, no one knows. I like to think that he joined his love.

The style of these Tibetan poems is simple, but tricky, and often humorous. They may or may not all have Tantric meanings. Some obviously do. If these poems were not written by the Sixth Dalai Lama, then we do not know who wrote them. He is remembered as the author by present-day Tibetans. And, it is my sincere hope that these little poems may be enjoyed by reader in the West. Perhaps they will open up Tibet to the western mind as something other than 'strange'.

I would like to acknowledge help given me by Thubten Norbu, the former Abbot of Kumbum, elder brother of the present Dalai Lama, and one of my Tibetan teachers and friends. Many interpretations of difficult colloquial expressions are his. Since many consider his brother to be a reincarnation of the author of these poems every shade of meaning was important to establish. He has helped me much.

These poems and the Sixth Dalai Lama remind me of my own religious struggles. I hope they mean something to every reader.

G.W.H.

INTRODUCTION

Tsangyang Gyatso (1983-1706), the sixth incarnation of the Bodhisattva Avalokiteshvara, the all-compassionate patron of Tibet, has been called by Professor Petech[1] "one of the finest poets of Tibet, nay, the only erotic poet of that country". For different reasons this poet has always attracted the interest of the West. The less genuine information existing on this talented but unfortunate youth, the more the unrestrained, sensation-bound imagination of western writers and journalists indulged in descriptions of the young Dalai Lama's personality from various approaches. Thus, the problem of Tsangyang Gyatso has been dealt with in several travel books by journalists who were afforded the opportunity to visit Tibet shortly before the forcible occupation of that unfortunate country by the Chinese communists (beginning in 1950). This is well known among our contemporaries, but it is hardly known beyond the circles of professors of literary history that as early as 1833, a representative of the radical-liberal writers of the school called "Young Germany", Karl Gutzkone, published a novel in two volumes called *Maha Guru.* In this novel the life of the young Dalai Lama (about which the author knew practically nothing) served as pretext for the explanation of his political ideas, and as an opportunity for slandering religion in general. Certainly the geographical inaccessibility of Tibet, corroborated by the interest of the successive Chinese governments since the K'ang-hsi era (1661-1722), made Tibet an isolated and "forbidden" country. This furnishes us an explanation for the total inaccessibility of reliable sources written in the original language. Therefore, several dubious writers felt encouraged to write about things Tibetan, preferably, on what they called the "wisdom of the east". The situation has changed since 1959 when the present Dalai Lama found asylum in India. There have been

1. Luciano Petech, *China and Tibet in the Early 18th Century*, (*Leiden*, 1950).

85,000 refugees who follow his example. Thanks to the numerous Tibetan refugee printing offices, which have been gradually established in India, valuable materials have now become accessible to serious western scholars.

The first publication of the "Love Songs" of Tsangyang Gyatso, accompanied by a translation, appeared in 1933.[1] This translation suffers from a lack of adequate materials concerning the songs, as well as reliable biographical texts. This is more reason to appreciate that Dr. G.W. Houston has decided to produce a new translation based upon an original Tibetan block-print. The translation of these poems was by no means an easy task, because the poems—like a good deal of other oriental poetry in Sanskrit, Chinese, Arabic, etc.—have often two, three, or even more layers of meaning. The language, though highly artistic, uses vocabulary from both the classical, literary language and the colloquial language of the 17th and 18th centuries. Some of these poems, or songs, expressing religious ideas may—but, not necessarily must—show an erotic second meaning. But, there is an undeniable Tantric (i.e., "Diamond Vehicle") touch. These facts reflect the ambiguity of Dalai Lama's behaviour. Tsangyang Gyatso's Tantric inclination becomes clear by two of his own writings which contain the Tantric propitiation of the terrible "Protector of the Buddhist doctrine" Tamdin (Hayagrīva). The amount of his literary work is understandably very small because of the Dalai Lama's early death.

An oral tradition is still alive that the houses of Zho, the village below the Potala palace where the young Dalai Lama met his sweethearts, are marked by yellow dye, while others are whitewashed. So, our great task will be devoted to the clarification of whether the Dalai Lama was a mere libertine or an adherent of a Tantric erotic cult, perhaps, even a shady one. It is now indispensable to adduce a few illustrations from the available historical and biographical sources.

Sumpa Khampo (1704-1776), a decided, high-spirited partisan of the Gelugpa school, whose leader is the respective

1. Yu Dawchyuan and Jaw Yuanrenn, *Love Songs of the Sixth Dalai-Lama*, Academia Sinica Series A No. 5. (Peiping, 1930).

incarnation of the Dalai Lama, wrote a short notice concerning the Sixth Dalai Lama in his *History of Buddhism in India, Tibet and Mongolia* :[1]

> "Then Tsangyang Gyatso, who was born into the family of the 'treasure discoverer' Padma Lingba of insane descent, took his novice vows from the Panchen Rimpoche. Although he remained on the (Potala) throne, he went (later) to Tashilhunpo and returned his vows to the Panchen Rimpoche, either because of the general deterioration of Tibet's virtue, or because of some circumstances. While he still retained secular power, which he did not want, and his father-in-law was regent, certain events occurred. The (Khoshot) King Lhabzang, who had been expelled (as stated above) by the regent, conducted war upon the regent. The regent, who had only a few followers, was eventually killed. After that, Tsangyang Gyatso, who had been invited to China, died on the road at a place in the Koko Nor area."

For a better understanding of this very concise statements of the historian, we must further examine evidence from other sources. Evidence is offered by the index volume of the Lhasa edition of the Kanjur[2] and the *Secret Biography of the sixth Dalai Lama.*[3] There is also an "Ordinary Biography" which is found in the first volume of the *Collected Works* of the Seventh Dalai Lama. The Ordinary Biography deals preferably with outer events of Tsangyang Gyatso's life. For the time being, it is not accessible to me, but the outward history can easily be presumed from other sources. The secret Biography, devoted to the spiritual life of the young hierarch with data about his most influential teachers, etc., proves to be more useful for our present purposes. A careful examination of the shorter description in the *Kanjur* index volume proves that it relies upon the Secret Biography almost literally. For this introduction, it will do to

1. Sumpa Mkhan-po, *Pag Sam Jon Zang*, ed. by Sarat Chandra Das, Part 2, (Calcutta, 1908), p. 30, lines 3-8.
2. Paktayā, Vol. 1, foll. 381a. 6ff.
3. *The Secret Biography of the Sixth Dalai Lama,* (text), reproduced by Ngawang Gelek Demo, (New Delhi, 1970).

quote the abridged description in the *Kanjur* index volume. The short remarks of Sumpa Khampo concerning the complicated political framework will become clearer once we examine the date from the *Kanjur* index volume.

One aspect of the problem should be stressed : the very angry attack of Sumpa Khampo on the "treasure (hidden books) discoverer" Padma Lingba, of whose family the Sixth Dalai Lama was a scion. The attack proves to be a general assault upon the old school of Tibetan Buddhism, the Nyingmapa, which goes back to the Indian masters Padmasambhava and Vimalamitra. The Nyingmapa is, in many ways, considered controversial and heretical by some orthodox Gelugpa. Sumpa Khampo's attack has inspired several "apologies" or "refutations" (rtsod-pai lan) from the side of the blamed school, in defense of their own teaching and Padma Lingba.

This is my translation of the remarks about the Sixth Dalai Lama as found in the *Kanjur* index volume : "The birth country of the sixth in the exalted lineage, the Victorious Lord,[1] the Omniscient Tsangyang Gyatso, was the hidden country Yul-sum, below Tsona, situated at the flank of Khampajong. There he was born in a supernatural way as the son of his father Rigdzin Tashi and his mother Tsewang Lhamo. This was in the water-pig year (1683). At that time there were immeasurable omens such as the rising of twelve suns. He dwelt in complete secrecy for a period of one year. In the ninth month of the fire-ox year (1697), he took the vows of renunciation of the world (pravrajita), in the presence of the omniscient, all-seeing Panchen Lozang Yeshe, the Vinaya teacher Yangdragpa, Kharegpa, Zilnon Dorje (the abbot of Ganden : Choni Tsultrim, and Geleg Gyatso).[2] He was given the name Omniscient Precious Tsangyang Gyatso. He studied spiritual texts like the Mañjuśrī Nāmasaṅgīti. At the twenty-fifth day of the tenth Mongol month (of the same year) he became enthroned in the Potala

1. Rgyal-dbang, the original title of the Gelubpa Avalokiteshvara incarnations : Dalai Lama is a Mongol title which was bestowed upon the third hierarch in 1578 by the Mongol ruler Altan Khan.

2. The bracketed names of these teachers have been added from the "Secret Biography", folio 22.3,4.

palace on the high golden throne, and received homage as protector of the whole people of Lhasa, and commander in-chief of the army. After his initiation, the Panchen Tozang Yeshe, the abbot of Banden Tsutrim Dargya, the monk Jamynag tag-pa, and his master Geleg Gyatso gave to him innumerable spiritual precepts and instructions. He learned metaphysics, and studied properly "the Purifying of the Mind" (sbyong) from the doctor (Rabjamba) Chagpa Chopel, and other excellent spiritual advisors. When the time came that (the Dalai Lama) followed additionally the religious discipline of the northern direction, there was, because of circumstances, disagreement between the regent and the King, Lhabzang. As the effect of the whole Tibetan people's low virtue increased, (the regent and Lhabzang) met for battle. Consequently, the great regent died. When messengers of the Chinese Emperor arrived, the manifold words of Lhabzang caused mishap. The Dalai Lama was ordered to go to China in the fire-pig year, when he was twenty-five years old (1707) (according to Professor Petech, 1706). Continuing his journey through Yangchen (south of the Tengri Nor), he reached the Upper Sog Country (to the northeast of the Tengri Nor). When the "invited" (party) was violently blamed by (the emissaries of) the Chinese emperor, he did not know what to do. When (Tsangyang Gyatso) was entreated by the accompanying party, he changed his mind (gave up his heretical religion ?). According to the not ordinary biography (="Secret Biography") he made this change known by a beautiful song, accompanying himself on the strings of his divine lute."

This seems to be a very moving description of the desolate young Dalai Lama, playing and singing a sad tune pervaded by his hopeless loneliness. The Secret Biography makes clear, that in a thick fog he lost the communication with his entourage. Tsepon W.W. Shakabpa,[1] who had access to other Tibetan sources, states that the Dalai Lama died at the Kunga Nor, a small lake south of the Koko Nor. Most sources state that he died because of a disease, but he might as well have been killed

1. Tsepon W.D. Shakabpa, *Tibet : A Political History* (New Haven and London, 1967), P. 133.

by murderers sent by his enemies. In this case, certainty seems not to be possible.

In order to acquire a better understanding of the hapless life of the Sixth Dalai Lama, it seems imperative to reconstruct the political and religious developments of this whole time period. The great Fifth Dalai Lama, Ṅgawang Gyatso, the actual founder of Tibetan theocracy, had reached his goal in 1642 with the help of the Khoshot ruler Gushri Khan. The latter became the protector and "patron" of the Gelugpa controlled Tibetan state. Because of the weakness of his successors, the Dzungar, a West Mongol group converted to Buddhism later than the Eastern Mongols, became the paramount and most warlike Inner Asian power. The Eastern Mongols converted by the third Gelugpa hierarch, Sonam Gyatso, gradually surrendered to the Manchus. Eventually, when the Manchus were able to overthrow the already tottering Ming dynasty of China, a completely new situation emerged which was to have a direct impact upon the developments of Tibet. The K'ang-hsi emperor (since 1661) the greatest of the Manchu rulers, adopted a policy of backing the Gelugpa, but also of making his influence felt in Tibet itself. He wanted to use the civilizing qualities of the Gelugpa school to avoid further unrest among the Mongols. He had been concerned about the awe-inspiring and increasing power of the Dzungars. At the north-western frontier, even after a defeat of the Dzungar Khan Galdan, things remained dangerous under Galdan's successor Tsewang Rabtan (since 1697). The entire situation worsened for Tibet as the Fifth Dalai Lama, in his last years, retired from worldly business and installed Sanggya Gyatso as regent (sde-srid). The latter was a very able ruler and highly learned author of many books, but he showed a decided inclination to the unreformed Nyingmapa school. He wanted cooperation with the Dzungars in worldly affairs. This fact set the K'ang-hsi emperor ill at ease.

Now, it is true, that the Dzungars also favoured the Gelugpa school, and were as shocked by the behaviour of the young Dalai Lama as was the K'ang-hsi emperor. But, on the other hand, the situation at Lhase invited them to follow their trend for expansion and display of military power using the Dalai Lama's life style as an invitation to interfere.

The Nyingmapa influence upon the Golugpa establishment dated back to the Great Fifth, among whose teachers had been several Nyingmapa monks. Therefore, it seems not surprising that while in secular affairs the Great Fifth followed a strict tendency of strengthening Gelugpa supremacy, he nevertheless kept a keen interest in the Nyingmapa teachings. His complete works include not less than four volumes of Nyingmapa writings which later were sealed. These were accessible to a Gelugpa for study only with special permission, very rarely granted. This inclination for Nyingmapa teaching increased with the regent Sanggya Gyatso, whose numerous and bulky literary works reveal an exorbitant knowledge of the teachings not only of the Nyingmapa and of other unreformed Buddhist schools, but even of the non-Buddhist Bonpo. The matter which most upset the Chinese emperor was the fact that the regent hid the death of Fifth Dalai Lama (1682), pretending that the Fifth was retired in meditation. Meanwhile, the regent had found the sixth incarnation, the later Tsangyang Gyatso, who was educated in secrecy. The Chinese emperor, who was a decided Gelugpa, also minded that the Sixth Dalai Lama had been born into a family which descended from the Nyingmapa "treasure discoverer" Padma ling-pa. This fact had led to the outburst of anger in Sumpa Khampo's *History of Buddhism* quoted above.

We are informed in detail by a source, which we would think least to produce clear-cut data on a religious scandal, about the heretical worship of Tsangyang Gyatse and his inner circle. This scandal which was much more aggravation than one or another love affair, and the matrimonial bonds with the daughter of the regent is found in a report by an army commander. It is a report of the Manchu general Funingga, the commander of a Chinese-Manchu force, ordered to be on the alert against the suspected aggression of the Dzungar Khan Tsewang Rabtan. This document is based upon information of Lhabzang of the Khan of the Khoshot, the grandson of Gushri Khan. Lhabzang Khan had attacked and killed the Tibetan regent in 1705, and his emissaries investigated the incriminating religious activities of the young Dalai Lama. The document has come down to us in the Manchu language,[1] but the occurrence of Mongol words shows that Lhabzang's information, which he had presented as an enemy of the Dalai Lama, has been literally translated from Mongol into Manchu. I shall translate here only the facts concerning the Dalai Lama's religious misbehaviour, and leave alone other, especially military, information.

"It has been said that at the time of Khri-srong lde-btsan[2] and the abbot Bodhisattva,[3] that the form of Padmasambhava's religion was in agreement with the *Yellow Doctrine* (Gelugpa). But when the writings of the later Padmasambhava and the earlier Padmasambhava were mixed in the books which were discovered from the hidden monk community of the *Red Doctrine*, it was said, that they did not agree . . .Although it is called the sacrament of the Dhāraṇī, there is no restriction (of intercourse) between mother and son, and between father and daughter. Although one calls it the scriptures of the Dhāraṇīs, it has been handed down from a truly heretical religion. There are paintings on which Śākyamuni Buddha is depicted as being shot with arrows, struck and stabbed. The Dharmapāla[4] (protector of the Doctrine) is looked upon as equal to the Buddha. (The informants) stated that there were many heretical things such as offering up (the symbols of) the privy parts of men and women . . .calling it the religion of the gTer-ston Padma gLing-pa, they

1. The Manchu reports of general Funingga have been edited and translated from the original manuscript by Eva S. Kraft, *Zum Dsungarekrieg in 18. Jahrhundert. Berichte des Generals Funingga*, (Leipzig. 1953). The translation of the passages of value for our present study is to be found pp. 65-67, the text transcription pp. 147-148. The passages concerning the Dalai Lama represent the weakest part of Dr. Kraft's translation. This is because of her insufficient knowledge of Buddhist matters. Therefore, I have had to prepare a new translation of the deciding passages.

2. Berke siturho han=Mongol : Berke śidurghu śiregetu qan, cp. C.F. Koeppen, *Die Religion des Buddha und ihre Entstehung*, (Berlin, 1906), Vol, 2, Die lamaische Hierarchie und Kirche, p. 108.

3. The abbot Bodhisattva is the famous Indian Buddhist teacher Shāntirakshita who had been invited by Khri-srong lde-btsan.

4. Manchu coicong=Tib. chos-skyong; a Dharmapāla like Mahākāla and Yamāntaka.

did it secretly at Meruling.[1] Following that religion, his Holiness the Dalai Lama has acted likewise. . . (The Dalai Lama, or his secret Group said) that which is called the Dhāraṇī religion belongs to the genuine religion, Having been established at Namgyā Ratsang,[2] the religion of the later Padmasambhava is being spread. . . (An informant hostile to the controversial worship said :) 'As to people who consider (their) religion identical with the religion of our Padmasambhava, do they not feign it while destroying the religion of our Padmasambhava ? Is it not a shameful guilt when they destroy the religion of our vow, the personal words of the Buddha and the offering of (our) minds ? Is it not a crime and a deplorable thing[3] for the holy scriptures ? . . . I have seen them and know them, and I do not speak in a deceiving way.' As a criterion of that, it can be said, that everybody knows (that the Dalai Lama) took the daughter of the regent as his wife. . . There (in Namgya Ratsang) happened manifold things, for instance, they took women. Even in their scriptures exist the initiations, secret instruction and the magic of the heretical white cap. Furthermore, they are taught the offerings (of symbols) of the privy parts of men and women. . . They have called their heretical religion the Dhāraṇī religion of the later Padmasambhava, which has been handed down from the white cap (sect). Furthermore, my men, who have gone there and returned, have seen that (the heretics) had destroyed the canopy of small Jo-bo (Buddha statue) and the foot insteps and flanks of the great Jo-bo. As to that, they have said to every-

1. A monastery in the north-eastern quarter of Lhasa (Tib. rMe-ru-gling). A. Ferrari, "Mkhyen-brtse's Guide to the Holy Places of Central Tibet', Serie Orientale Roma XVI, (Rome, 1958), p.41 (here written rMar-ru, pronounced Mcru) and p. 94 (note 70).

2. Manchu Namja Razang, Tib. Namgyal Dratsang (or Ratsang) called also, rNam-rgyal Chos-sde. Cp. Ferrari, loc. cit., p. 110. This religious institution is the private monastery of the Dalai Lama in the Potala.

3. E. Kraft does not translate the word *motak*, which is obviously not Manchu, but most probably is a Middle Iranian word. The Middle Iranian word was probably borrowed first by the Uighurs, who have handed it down to rhw Mongols. Modak (M. Iranian) means "lamentation, something deplorable", trouble H.S. Nyberg, *A Manual of Pahlavi*, Part 2: Glossary, (Wiesbaden, 1974), p. 133.

body that it was the destruction by the "Roaring Bull" (the God of the Dead)."[1]

The document quoted above is indubitably a "trouvaille" of the highest importance. The main point must be seen in the fact that here we are dealing with primary information which in the regests (Chinese : Shih-lu) of the K'ang-hsi era will appear only, if at all, the form of a few condensed sentences which blame Tsangyang Gyatso, as a monk not worthy of his high position. The details of no interest to the Chinese annalists have been suppressed. Also, the Secret Biography, if studied thoroughly (which is my intention), is not likely to go beyond a few hints, because the decorum of the Gelugpa establishment would hardly allow these unusual facts to become known in detail.

The Manchu document answers the main question at the beginning of our considerations : the Sixth Dalai Lama was not a mere libertine, but the center of secret Nyingmapa Tantric circle. The details make it clear that we do not meet with ordinary Nyingmapa Tantric mysticism and magic. But, with a doctrine and practice, severely condemned by the reformer Atīsha in the eleventh century, and later by the founder of the Gelugpa school, the great Tsongkhapa. The Tantrism described in the document makes it obvious that the young Dalai Lama had turned to a ritual which completes the consummation of the united macrocosmic and microcosmic polarity, not as would be the usual way by acts of imagination, but turned into palpable sexual magic. Besides, there are some embarrassing hints to sinister tendencies, if we remember that the participants of the ritual had pictures in their room which displayed shooting, striking and stabbing of the Buddha. Also, the damage inflicted upon the two most sacred Buddha statues of Lhasa, the two Jo-bo, undoubtedly make obvious a sinister tendency, and this destructive activity is ascribed by them to the god of hell. This statement should mean, most probably, a conjuration of the evil god, a fact bringing Tsangyang Gyatso near to something

1. Oker dagorisukci = Mongol, oker dagurisugci, the Lord of the Lower world (Tib. gShin rje, Sanskrit Yama). This god stands on a bull, and has a bull's head. See A. Getty, *The Gods of Northern Buddhism*, (Rutland, Vermont : 1962), p. 153. (The Gsang-sgrub form) is found on plate 46a.

like a Buddhist "satanism". This seems to be very strange contrasting the tenderness and delicate feelings expressed in his poems. However, we should not forget that the negative rituals are dated 1705 and 1706, a very short time before the Dalai Lama's death in the Koko Nor region. And furthermore, it seems certain that the group of men who were present when he took his vows included as sNgags-pa, a magician, called the Master Jamyang Chophel (Secret Biography, folio 22, lines 2-3). The young hierarch was probably surrounded by Nyingmapa teachers very early, as it was the case with his predecessor.

The texts contain another subject of highest importance. I refer to "the later Padmasambhava's teachings", which are very clearly denoted as the source of the heretical influence on the Dalai Lama. The "later Padmasambhava" must have taught different religious conceptions that the "earlier Padmasambhava" the apostle of Tantric Buddhism, who had been invited to Tibet in the second half of the eighth century by the emperor Khri-srong lde-btsan to remove the impediments to the introduction of Buddhism. And even more, our texts furnish us with unequivocal information telling us that the "later Padmasambhava" was the discoverer of treasures" (gTer-ma), hidden according to the Nyingmapa books by the earlier Padmasambhava, or some of his disciples, to be discovered at a later time by inspired men whose names are given in the prophecies of events in the biography of the old Padmasambhava. It is evident that the biography contains quite a few later additions. The later Padmasambhava has been identified in the Manchu text with Padma gLing-pa (born 1490). This man, according to Sumpa Khampo and the account given in the Kanjur index volume, was the ancestor of Tsangyang Gyatso. It seems that the tradition of his family was reclaimed by Padma gLing-pa's scion. We must assume, from the sources quoted, that the gTer-ston introduced, nay, foisted teachings to the original Nyingmapa doctrines, and that he took these teachings, as the text states, from "the heretical white cap".

We run into considerable difficulties with this term. We know that, in general, the Gelugpa are known to wear yellow caps, as do the Nyingmapa. The Karmapa school had two lineages of incarnated lamas, one of them the "Red

Cap Karmapa" (Zhamar Karmapa) which was suppressed during the last quarter of the eighteenth century, the other being the "Black Hat Karmapa" (Zhanag Karmapa), still active till the present day. The non-Buddhist Bonpo, it is true, use white caps occasionally, but only on special occasions. White hats are not representative for that religion. Besides, the sources would have mentioned a Bonpo influence as a useful argument for the adversaries to blame Padma gLing-pa, as well as the Sixth Dalai Lama. "White Caps" have been mentioned also by the Mongol historian Sanang Secen, alias Secen Saghang, as inhabitants of the town of Hami during the time that Dayan Khaghan (1470-1543) was the most important Mongol ruler.[1] Hami is situated not very far to the east of the Turfan oasis. Unitl 1250, this was the center of the Uighur kingdom where, besides the Buddhist religious majority, also some Manichaeans were dwelling. As Padma gLing-pa and Dayan Khagan were contemporaries, it seems at least worthwhile to assume hypothetically that the "White Caps" would be brought into connection with a small group of possibly degenerate adherents of that religion. In my *Religions of Tibet* (London, 1961, p. 179), I tentatively connected the heresy of the Sixth Dalai Lama, or rather of Padma gLing-pa, with a sort of Manichaean infilteration into the Nyingmapa doctrine. It certainly was a typical and well-known method of the Manichaeans, from the very beginning, to speak to adherents of other religions in their own peculiar terminology : to Iranians in Zoroastrian, to the Christian peoples of the Mediterranian in Christian, and to the Buddhist population of Eastern Turkestan in Buddhist terms. The Manichees, when officially suppressed, managed to survive in different areas as underground movements, for instance in a sect in the Chinese province Fu-kien, as the so-called Bogomils

1. I.J. Schmidt. *Geschichte der Ost-Mongolen und ihres Furstenhauses verfasst von Ssanang Ssetsen Chungtaidschi*, (St. Petersburg, 1829), pp. 192-193, and p. 408 (note 34). Schmidt does not believe that the "White Caps" (caghan malaghai) of Hami (Mongol Khami; Turkic Khomul) are a tribe, but rather a religious sect. He feels it unlikely that the name applies to the Muslims of that area. There were only a few of these who made the pilgrimage to Mecca, and they wore a white turban. On the other hand, his assumption that this term might apply to some Indian sect seems to be quite improbable for the time of Dayan Khaghan.

and Cathari in areas of the Byzantine empire and Bulgaria, and in Southern France and Northern Italy, respectively.[1] Also, in this connection, a passage of Padmasambhava's preaching in different ways to different peoples, described in my *Religions of Tibet* (pp. 58,59) seems to be of interest.

The term denoting the Sixth Dalai Lama's heresy, in the *Kanjur* index volume and in the secret Biography, is not the "Doctrine of the White Cap", but "the discipline of the northern direction." For an elucidation of this term an article of Li An-che, "Rñiṅma-pa : the Early Form of Lamaism" (*JRAS* 1948-1950, pp. 149ff) will be helpful. We learn that there was both a "Southern Treasures School" and a "Northern Treasures School. The southern school disseminated from the monastery sMin grol-gling to the east of the Yarlung area. The northern school's teachings were practices at Dorjetrak, situated on the northern bank of the river Tsangpo, half-way between Samya (Bsam yas) and the issue of the Kyichu; and at Ka-thog in rDzachukha, south of the Derge district. This latter school should be identical with "the discipline of the northern direction", to which the Sixth Dalai Lama was given.

I hope that the evidence I have adduced in the introduction has made the problem of Tsangyang Gyatso's heresy somewhat more intelligible, as well as giving some information on the author of these poems. The definite and exhaustive answer to many questions and remaining uncertainties will mostly come from the gTer-ma books of Padma gLing-pa. I see forward to this subject by the means of a more technical philological study in the future.

H.H.

1. Dmitri Obolensky, *The Bogomils*, (Twickenham, Middlesex, 1972), Arno Borst, *Die Katharer*, Stuttgart, 1953).

1

ཤར་ཕྱོགས་རི་བོའི་རྩེ་ནས།
དཀར་གསལ་ཟླ་བ་ཤར་བྱུང་།
མ་སྐྱེས་ཨ་མའི་ཞལ་རས།
ཡིད་ལ་འཁོར་འཁོར་བྱས་བྱུང་།

Śar phyogs ri bo'i rtse nas
dkar gsal zla ba śar byung/
ma skyes a ma'i źal ras/
yid la 'khor 'khor byas byung/

Behind peaks of eastern mountains
The shining white moon appears,
And one girl's face
Turns round in my mind.

2

ན་ཉིང་བཏབ་པས་ལྗང་གཞོན།
ད་ལོ་སོག་མའི་ཕོན་ལྕོག།
ཕོ་གཞོན་རྒྱས་པས་ལུས་པོ།
ལྷོ་གཞུ་དེ་ལས་གྱོང་བ།

na ning btab pas ljang gźon/
da lo sog ma'i phon lcog[1]/
pho gźon rgyas[2] pas lus po/
lho gźu de las gyong[3] ba[4]/

Last year grain was sown;
This year stalks are blown.
A young man's frame has grown
Taut as a southern bow.*

1. Das: lcag
2. Das : rgas
3. read : rgyong
4. Das : ba'i

*To the south of Tibet, Bhutan and other countries is where bamboo grows. This bamboo is famous for making bows. Charles Bell, *Tibet : Past and Present.* (Oxford. 1924). Also, Shakabpa reminds us that Tshangs dbyangs rgya mtsho (Tsangyang Gyatso), the Sixth Dalai Lama was an excellent archer. Tsepon W. D. Shakabpa. *Tibet : A Political History.* (New Haven and London. 1957).

3

རང་སེམས་སོང་བའི་མི་དེ།
གཏན་གྱི་མདུན་མར་བྱུང་ན།
རྒྱ་མཚོའི་གཏིང་ནས་ནོར་བུ།
ལོན་པ་དེ་དང་མཉམ་བྱུང་།

rang sems song ba'i mi de/
gtan[1] gyi mdun mar byung na/
rgya mtsho'i gting nas nor bu/
lon pa de dang mnyam byung/

If the one I love
May stay with me,
How like the jewel from
Beneath the sea.

1. Das : brtan

4

འགྲོ་ཞོར་ལམ་པའི་སྙིང་ཐུབ།
ལུས་དྲི་ཞིམ་པའི་བུ་མོ།
གཡུ་ཆུང་གྲུ་དཀར་བརྙེད་ནས།
སྐྱུར་བ་དེ་དང་འདྲ་བྱུང་།

'gro źor lam pa'i[1] snying thub/
lus dri źim pa'i bu mo/
g-yu chung gru dkar brnyed[2] nas/
skyur ba de dang 'dra byung/

Meeting along the way
This sweetly smelling girl,
Fine small white turquoise
Found, then cast away.

1. Das : bu'i
2. Das : rnyed

5

མི་ཆེན་དཔོན་པོའི་སྲས་མོ།
ཁམས་འབྲས་མཚར་ལ་བལྟས་ན།
ཁམ་སྡོང་མཐོན་པོའི་རྩེ་ན།
འབྲས་བུ་སྨིན་པ་འདྲ་བྱུང་།

mi chen dpon po'i sras mo/
khams 'bras mtshar la bltas na/
kham sdong mthon po'i rtse na/
'bras bu smin pa 'dra byung/

Admiring a princess
Fair as a peach,
Ripened fruit,
Atop the tall tree.

6

སེམས་པ་ཕར་ལ་ཤོར་ནས།
མཚན་མོའི་གཉིད་ཐེབས་གཅོག་གི།
ཉིན་མོ་ལག་ཏུ་མ་ལོན།
ཡིད་ཐང་ཆད་རོགས་ཡིན་པ།

sems pa phar la śor nas/
mtshon mo'i gnyid thebs gcog gi/
nyin mo lag tu ma lon/
yid thang chad rogs yin pa/

My mind roams by day;
I cannot sleep at night.
Daily affairs have no end;
Fatigue is my only friend.

མེ་ཏོག་ནམ་ཟླ་ཡལ་སོང་།
གཡུ་སྦྲང་སེམས་པ་མ་སྐྱོ།
བྱམས་པ་ལས་འཕྲོ་ཟད་པས།
ང་ནི་སྐྱོ་རྒྱུ་མི་འདུག།

me tog nam zla yal song/
g-yu sbrang sems pa ma skyo/
byams pa las 'phro zad pas/
nga ni skyo rgyu mi 'dug/

The season of flowers has passed,
The turquoise bee does not grieve.
Spent by love, nor have I
Any season of sadness.

8

རྩི་ཐོག་བ་མོའི་ཁ་ལ།
སྐྱེ་སེར་རླུང་གི་ཕོ་ཉ།
མེ་ཏོག་སྦྲང་བུ་གཉིས་ཀྱི།
འབྲེལ་མཚམས་བྱེད་མཁན་ལོས་ཡིན།

rtsi thog ba mo'i kha la/
skye[1] ser rlung gi pho nya/
me tog sbrang bu gnyis kyi/
'brel mtshams byed mkhan los yin/

Hoarfrost on late fruit,
Messenger of winter wind.
Flower and bee
He parts from each other.

1. Das : skyeng

9

ངང་པ་འདམ་ལ་ཆགས་ནས།
རེ་ཞིག་སྡོད་དགོས་བསམས་ཀྱང་།
མཚོ་མོ་དར་ཁ་འགྲིགས་ནས།
རང་སེམས་ཁོ་ཐག་ཆོད་སོང་།

ngang pa 'dam la chags nas/
re źig sdad dgos bsams kyang/
mtsho mo dar kha 'grigs[1] nas/
rang sems kho thag chod song/

Marsh-loving geese
Wished to stay,
Icy despair
Sped them on their way.

1. Das : bsgrigs

10

གྲུ་ཤན་སེམས་པ་མེད་ཀྱང་།
རྟ་མགོས་ཕྱི་མིག་བལྟས་བྱུང་།
འཁྲིལ་གཟུང་མེད་པའི་བྱམས་པས།
ང་ལ་ཕྱི་མིག་མི་ལྟ།

gru śan sems pa med kyang/
rta mgos phyi mig bltas byung/
khril[1] bzung med pa'i byams pas/
nga la phyi mig mi lta/

The figurehead horse
On a senseless ferry
Turns back and stares;
My shameless lover
Glances not toward me.

1. Das : khrel; read: 'khril

11

ཆུང་འདྲིས་བྱམས་པའི་རླུང་བསྐྱེད།
ལྕང་མའི་ལོགས་ལ་བཙུགས་ཡོད།
ལྕང་སྲུང་ཨ་ཇོ་ཞལ་ངོས།
རྡོག་གྲ་རྒྱབ་པ་མ་གནང་།

chung 'dris byams pa'i rlung bskyed/
lcang ma'i logs la btsugs yod/
lcang srung a jo źal ngos/
rdog gra rgyab pa ma gnang/[1]

Playmates so dear, we hoisted
Prayerflags beside a willow tree;
Forest keeper Ajo sengo*
Don't kick in anger at me.

1. Das : rdo ka rgyag pa ma gnang/

*Tibetan : a jo źal ngo

12

བྲིས་པའི་ཡི་གེ་ནག་ཆུང་།
ཆུ་དང་ཐིག་པས་བཤིག་སོང་།
མ་བྲིས་སེམས་ཀྱི་རི་མོ།
བསུབས་ཀྱང་ཟུབ་རྒྱུ་མི་འདུག །

bris pa'i yi ge nag chung/
chu dang thig pas bśig[1] song/
ma bris sems kyi ri mo/
bsubs[2] kyang zub[3] rgyu mi 'dug/

Small written letters
Destroyed by water drops.
Unwritten memories
Never could be so erased.

1. Das : 'jigs
2. Das : sub

13

རྒྱབ་པའི་ནག་ཆུང་ཐེའུས།
གསུང་སྐད་འབྱོན་ནི་མི་ཤེས།
ཁྲེལ་དང་གཞུང་གི་ཐེའུ།
སོ་སོའི་སེམས་ལ་སྐྱོན་དང་།

rgyab pa'i[1] nag chung the'us/
gsung skad 'byon ni mi śes/
khrel dang gźung gi the 'u/
so so'i sems la skyon dang/

I do not know the words
Stamped here in black;
The small seal stands blameless,
There is fault in every mind.

1. Das : pas

14

སྟོབས་ལྡན་ཧ་ལོའི་མེ་ཏོག།
མཆོད་པའི་རྫས་ལ་ཕེབས་ན།
གཡུ་སྦྲང་གཞོན་ནུ་ང་ཡང་།
ལྷ་ཁང་ནང་ལ་ཁྲིད་དང་།

stong[1] ldan ha lo'i me tog/
mchod pa'i rdzas la phebe na/
g-yu sbrang gźon nu nga yang/
lha khang nang la khrid dang/

You go to a place of honor,
A robust Halo* flower;
Come into the temple with me,
A youthful turquoise bee.

1. Das : stobs
*Tibetan : ha lo

15

སེམས་སོང་བུ་མོ་མི་བཞུགས།
དམ་པའི་ཆོས་ལ་ཕེབས་ན།
ཕོ་གཞོན་ང་ཡང་མི་སྡོད།
རི་ཁྲོད་བགྲིམ་ལ་ཐལ་འགྲོ།

sems song bu mo mi bźugs/
dam pa'i chos la phebs na/
pho gźon nga yang mi sdod/
ri khrod bgrim la thal 'gro/

If my love embraces
Holy Dharma, not me,
Soon my youth will be spent
In a mountain retreat.

16

མཚན་ལྡན་བླ་མའི་དྲུང་དུ།
སེམས་འཁྲིད་ཞུ་བར་ཕྱིན་པས།
སེམས་པ་འགོར་ཀྱང་མི་ཐུབ།
བྱམས་པའི་ཕྱོགས་ལ་ཤོར་སོང་།

tshad[1] ldan bla ma'i drung du/
sems 'khrid źu bar phyin pas/
sems pa 'gor kyang mi thub/
byams pa'i phyogs la śor song/

I went before my guru
Asking to be taught;
My mind always fought
Slipping back home to you.

1. Das : mtshan

17

བསྒོམས་པའི་བླ་མའི་ཞལ་རས།
ཡིད་ལ་ཡང་ཡང་ཤར་བྱུང་།
མ་སྒོམ་བྱམས་པའི་ཞལ་རས།
ཡིད་ལ་ཝ་ལེ་ཝ་ལེ།

bsgoms[1] pa'i bla ma'i źal ras/
yid la yang yang śar byung/[2]
. . .[3]

When meditating, I cannot retain
My guru's face to see;
Not meditating, I cannot restrain
My loved one's face in me.

1. Das : sgam
2. Das : yid la 'char rgyu mi 'dug/
3. Das : ma sgom byams pa'i źal ras /
   yid la va le vu (read : va) le /

18

སེམས་པ་འདི་ལ་འགྲོ་འགྲོ།
དམ་པའི་ཆོས་ལ་ཕྱིན་ན།
ཚེ་གཅིག་ལུས་གཅིག་ཉིད་ལ།
སངས་རྒྱས་ཐོབ་པ་འདུག་གོ

sems pa 'di la 'gro 'gro/
dam pa'i chos la phyin na/
tshe gcig lus gcig nyid la/
sangs rgyas thob pa 'dug go/

If one does live for Dharma
And does continue to do so,
One may become a Buddha
In yet this same lifetime.

དག་པ་ཤེལ་རི་གངས་ཆུ།
ཀླུ་བདུད་རྡོ་རྗེའི་ཟིལ་པ།
བདུད་རྩི་སྨན་གྱིས་ཕབ་རྒྱུན།
ཆང་མ་ཡེ་ཤེས་མཁའ་འགྲོ།
དམ་ཚིག་གཙང་མས་བཏུང་ན།
ངན་སོང་མྱོང་དགོས་མི་འདུག།

dag pa śel ri gangs chu/
klu bdud rdo rje'i zil pa/
bdud rtsi sman gyi[1] phab rgyun/
chang ma ye śes mkha' 'gro/
dam tshig gtsang mas btung na/
ngan song myong dgos mi 'dug/

Drops of Lu Du Dorjay,*
River from pure crystal mountain,
Flow down as herbal nectar;
Drinking gifts of the barmaid,
Ye she Khando,** with pureness,
One need not to suffer damnation.***

1. Das : gyis

*Tibetan : klu bdud rdo rje, a deity who is white in color and Rides on the horse of Klu spirits. R. de Nebesky-Wojkowitz, *Oracles and Demons of Tibet*, (The Hague, 1956).

**Tibetan : ye śes mkha 'gro.

***The symbolism of this entire poem is Tantric : The drops are identical with the river. In turn, the river is identical with the male semen which becomes amṛta, the drink of immortality when mixed with female blood. The offerings of the barmaid is this wine (blood). This poem is concerned with the Tantric union of the male and female polarities—ritual intercourse—which must be undertaken with a vow of purity in order to become useful to the yogin.

20

རླུང་རྟ་ཡར་འགྲོའི་དུས་ལ།
རླུང་བསྐྱེད་དར་ལྕོག་བཙུགས་པས།
མཛངས་མ་མ་བཟང་བུ་མོའི།
མགྲོན་པོ་ལ་ནི་བོས་བྱུང་།

rlung rta yar 'gro'i dus la/
rlung bskyed dar lcog[1] btsugs pas/
mdzangs[2] ma ma bzang bu mo'i/
mgron po la ni bos byung/

I raised a banner,
Silk flag blowing in the wind.
Mazang* the noble's daughter
Invited me home as a friend.

1. Das : lcag
2. Das : 'dzang

*Tibetan : ma bzang

21

སོ་དཀར་པགས་པའི་འཛུམ་མདངས།
བཞུགས་གྲལ་སྤྱི་ལ་བལྟས་ནས།
མིག་ཟུར་ཕྲ་མོའི་སྒྲིལ་མཚམས།
གཞོན་པའི་གདོང་ལ་བལྟས་བྱུང་།

so dkar pags[1] pa'i 'dzum mdangs/
bźugs gral spyi la bltas nas[2]
mig zur phra[3] mo'i sgril mtshams/
gźon pa'i gdong la bltas byung/

Seeing a row of seated maidens
All smiles and white teeth,
I catch one winking at me
From the corner of an eye.

1. Das : lpags
2. Das : na
3. Das : khra

22

ཧ་ཅང་སེམས་ལ་སོང་ནས།
འགྲོགས་འདྲིས་ཨེ་ཡོང་དྲིས་པས།
འཆི་བྲལ་བྱེད་ན་མིན་པ།
གསོན་བྲལ་མི་བྱེད་གསུངས་བྱུང་།

ha cang sems la song nas/
'grogs 'dris e yong dris pas/
'chi bral byed na min pa/
gson bral mi byed gsungs byung/

Falling in love, I asked:
"Will you come stay with me ?"
She replied indeed she would,
Until the day she died.

23

མཛངས་མའི་ཐུགས་དང་བསྟུན་ན།
ཚེ་འདིའི་ཆོས་སྐལ་ཆད་འགྲོ།
དབེན་པའི་རི་ཁྲོད་འགྲིམས་ན།
བུ་མོའི་ཐུགས་དང་འགལ་འགྲོ།

mdzangs[1] ma'i thugs dang bstun na/
tshe 'di'i[2] chos skal chad 'gro/
dben pa'i ri khrod 'grims na/
bu mo'i thugs dang 'gal 'gro/

My religious vows do not meet
Wishes of her heart;
If I go into retreat,
Her wishes must depart.

1. Das : 'dzang
2. Das : 'di

24

འཛུམ་དང་སོ་དཀར་སྟོན་ཕྱོགས།
གཞོན་པའི་བློ་ཁྲིད་ཡིན་འདུག
སྙིང་ནས་ཤ་ཚ་ཡོད་མེད།
དབུ་མནའ་བཞེས་རོགས་གནང་དང་།

'dzum[1] dang so dkar ston phyogs[2]/
gźon pa'i blo khrid yin 'dug/
. . .[3]
dbu mna' bźes[4] rogs gnang dang/

You smile, flashing white teeth.
I have no experience.
Please grant me first an oath,
And manifest compassion.

1. Das : mdzum
2. Das : chog
3. Das : snying nas śa tsha yod med/
4. Das : mnab źes

25

སྙིང་ཐུབ་ཡིད་འཕྲོག་ལྷ་མོ།
རྔོན་པ་རང་གིས་ཟིན་ཀྱང་།
དབང་ཆེན་མི་ཡི་དཔོན་པོ།
ནོར་བཟང་རྒྱལ་བུས་འཕྲོགས་སོང་།

snying thub yid 'phrog lha mo/
rngon pa rang gis[1] zin kyang/
dbang chen mi yi dpon po/
nor bzang rgyal bus[2] 'phrogs song/

I, the hunter, trapped
A fair lady, who
Was taken from me
By Norzang Jaybu*

1. Das : nga ras
2. Das : rgya lus
*Tibetan : Nor bzang rgyal bu

ནོར་བུ་རང་ལ་ཡོད་དུས། །
ནོར་བུའི་ནོར་ཉམས་མཆོད། །
ནོར་བུ་མི་ལ་ཤོར་དུས། །
སྙིང་རླུང་སྟོད་ལ་ཚངས་བྱུང་། །

nor bu rang la g-yod[1] dus/
nor bu'i nor nyams mchod[2]/
nor bu mi la śor dus/
snying rlung stod la tshangs[3] byung /

When one does own a gem,
Its value is not sublime;
But when it is taken from him,
Then soon the worth does climb.

1. Das: yod
2. Das: ma chod
3. Das: tshang

27

རང་ལ་དགའ་བའི་བྱམས་པ།
གཞན་གྱི་མདུན་མར་བླངས་སོང་།
ཁོང་ནང་སེམས་པའི་གཅོང་གིས།
ལུས་པོའི་ཤ་ཡང་བསྐམས་སོང་།

rang la dga' ba'i byams pa/
gźan gyi mdun mar blangs song/
khong[1] nang sems pa'i gcong gis/
lus po'i śa yang bskams[2] song/

My desired did part,
Becoming another's dear wife;
Weariness of my mind
Dries even my flesh away.

1. Das: khog
2. Das: skam

28

སྙིང་ཐུབ་རྐུ་ལ་ཤོར་སོང་།

མོ་ཕྱ་རྩིས་འབུལ་རན་སོང་།
བུ་མོ་དུང་སེམས་ཅན་མ།
རྨི་ལམ་ནང་ལ་འཁོར་སོང་།

snying thub rku la śor song/
mo phya[1] rtsis 'bul ran song/
bu mo dung sems can ma/
rmi lam nang la 'khor song/

Someone has stolen from me
That one with conch-white heart.
Astrologer, to you I come.
She still invades my dreams.

1. Das: cha

29

བུ་མོར་འཆི་བ་མེད་ན།
ཆང་ལ་འཛད་པ་མི་འདུག།
གཞོན་པའི་བརྟན་གྱིས་སྐྱབས་གནས།
འདི་ལ་བཅོལ་པས་ལོས་ཆོག།

bu mor 'chi ba med na/
chang la 'dzad pa mi 'dug/
gźon pa' igtan[1] gyis skyabs gnas/
'di la bcol pas los chog/

She must never be granted to die;
The wine is surely not spent.
This maiden is my refuge.
With her I rest content.

1. Das: brtan

བུ་མོ་ཨ་མར་མ་སྐྱེས།
ཁམ་བུའི་ལ་སྐྱེས་སམ།
ཨ་གསར་ཟད་པ་ཁམ་བུའི།
མེ་ཏོག་དེ་ལས་མགྱོགས་པ།

bu mo a mar ma skyes/
pham[1] bu'i śing las[2] skyes sam/
a gsar zad pa kham bu'i/
me tog de las mgyogs pa[3]/

Does indeed even she have a mother ?
Could it be on a tree she was born ?
Her love true that she held seems to fade,
So much sooner than the blossoms of peach.

1. Das: kham
2. Das: la
3. Das: pas

31

བུ་མོ་ཆུང་འདྲིས་བྱམས་པ།
སྤྱང་ཀིའི་རིགས་བརྒྱུད་མིན་ནམ།
ཤ་འདྲིས་ལྤགས་འདྲིས་བྱུང་ཡང་།
རི་ལ་ཡར་གྲབས་མཛད་ཀྱི།

bu mo chung 'dris byams pa/
spyang kyi'i[1] rigs brgyud min nam/
śa 'dris sbag'[2] dris byung yang[3]
ri la yol[4] grabs[5] mdzad kyi[6]/

Is my beloved playmate
Truly the wolf's cousin ?
She appears for meat and gravy,
Then to the mount again.

1. Das: gi'e; read: ki'i
2. Das: lpags
3. Das: kyang
4. Das: yar
5. Das: grab
6. Das: kyis

32

རྟ་རྒོད་རི་ལ་རྒྱབ་པ།
རྙེ་དང་ཞགས་པས་ཟིན་གྱིས།
བྱམས་པ་ངོ་ལོག་རྒྱབ་པ།
ཐུགས་ངོ་ཟིན་པ་མི་འདུག།

rta rgod[1] ri la[2] rgyab pa/
rnye[3] dang źags pas zin gyi[4]/
byams pa ngo log rgyab pa[5]/
thugs[6] ngo zin pa mi 'dug/

One holds with rope and beats
Unruly horses in mountains.
One may never hold near a heart
Of a love that does depart.

1. Das: rgad
2. Das: yar
3. Das: rnyi
4. Das: gyis
5. Das: pas
6. Das: mthu

33

བྲག་དང་རླུང་པོ་སྡེབས་ནས། །
རྒོད་པོའི་སྒྲོ་ལ་གཞན་བྱུང་། །
གཡོ་ཅན་རྫུ་བག་ཅན་གྱིས། །
ང་ལ་གཟན་པོ་བྱས་བྱུང་། །

brag dang rlung po sdebs nas/
rgod[1] po'i sgro la gzan[2] byung/
g-yo can rdzu bag can gyis/
nga la gzan[3] po byas byung/

I am weary of senate debate
Mixed with wind and rocks.
I am weary of sly craft gentlemen
Spotted by tainted smiling.

1. Das: rgad
2. Das: zan
3. Das: zan

34

སྤྲིན་པ་ཁ་སེར་གཏིང་ནག །
སད་དང་སེ་རའི་གཞི་མ །
བན་དེ་སྐྱ་མིན་སེར་མིན །
སངས་རྒྱས་བསྟན་པའི་དགྲ་བོ །

sprin pa kha ser gting nag/
sad dang se ra'i gźi ma/
ban de[1,2] skya min ser mi na[3]/
sangs rgyas bstan pa'i dgra bo/

Snowy cloud with dark inside
Is the home of frost and hail,
While the monk not white nor yellow,*
Is the foe of Buddha's teaching.

1. Das: dhe
2. read: ban dhe
3. Das: min

*The yellow refers to his clerical garb, while the white is a reference to his heart. The Tibetans call an honest person a white heart.

35

ས་དེ་ཁ་ཞུ་གཏིང་འཁུགས།
རྟ་ཕོ་གཏོང་ས་མ་རེད།
གསར་འགྲོགས་བྱམས་པའི་ཕྱོགས་སུ།
སྙིང་གཏམ་བཤད་ས་མ་རེད།

sa de kha źu[1] gting 'khugs[2]/
rta pho gtong sa ma red/
gsar 'grogs byams pa'i phyogs su/
snying gtam bśad sa ma red/

In a place of melting snow
With a creek hidden below,
This is not the place to loose your stallion.
Nor, should one betray a secret
To a newly found girl friend.

1. Das: bur (?)
2. Das : khug

36

ཚེས་ཆེན་བཅོ་ལྔའི་ཟླ་བ།
ཡིན་པ་འདྲ་བ་འདུག་སྟེ།
ཟླ་བའི་དཀྱིལ་གྱི་རི་བོང།
ཚེ་ཟད་ཚར་ནས་འདུག་གོ།

tshes chen bco lnga'i zla ba/
yin pa 'dra ba 'dug ste/
zla ba'i dkyil gyi ri bong/
tshe zad tshar nas 'dug go/

The fifteenth day of the month*
Is the greatest day.
The pious hare is in the moon,**
After a time consumed.

*Since the Tibetans use a lunar system for counting, this is the full moon day.

**This is in reference to a story of Buddha in a previous lifetime. "In the later post-Christian legends of the Buddha it is related that the Bodhisattva (Gautama) when born as a hare gave up his body vicariously. Indra out of wonder and curiosity carried him up to hevan for the purpose of showing him to the gods, and kept him on the orb of the moon that human beings might see him at all times. Since that time the moon became known as the holder of the pious hare." Sarat Chandra Das. *A Tibetan-English Dictionary*, (Delhi, reprint 1970). p. 1175b.

37

ཟླ་བ་འདི་ནས་ཕར་འགྲོ།
རྟིང་མའི་ཟླ་བ་ཚར་ཡོང་།
བཀྲ་ཤིས་ཟླ་བ་དཀར་པོ།
ཟླ་སྟོད་ཕྱོགས་ལ་མཇལ་ཡོང་།

zla ba 'di nas phar 'gro/
rting ma'i[1] zla ba tshar[2] yong[3]/
bkra śis zla ba dkar po/
zla stod phyogs la mjal yong/

After this moon elapses,
After one month we will meet.
Lucky white moon I do see,
In next moon's first part we will greet.

1. Das: gting ma'i
2. Das: tshur
3. Das: yongs

38

དབུས་ཀྱི་རི་རྒྱལ་ལྷུན་པོ།
མ་འགྱུར་བརྟན་པར་བཞུགས་དང།
ཉི་མ་ཟླ་བའི་བསྐོར་ཕྱོགས།
ནོར་ཡོང་བསམ་པ་མི་འདུག།

dbus kyi ri rgyal lhun po/
ma 'gyur brtan par bźugs dang/
nyi ma zla ba'i bskor phyogs/
nor yong bsam pa mi 'dug/

If Mount Meru does stand,*
And the sun and moon
Do revolve, this thought
May not be held false.

*This is not a physical mountain, but the central mountain of the universe. It also is the spinal cord of the meditating yogin.

39

ཚེས་གསུམ་ཟླ་བ་དཀར་བ།
དཀར་གོས་ནང་ནས་ཆོད་སོང་།
བཅོ་ལྔའི་ནམ་དང་མཉམ་པའི།
ཞལ་བཞེས་ཅིག་ཀྱང་གནང་ཞུ།

tshes gsum zla ba dkar ba/
dkar gos nang nas chod song/
bco lnga'i nam dang mnyam pa'i /
źal bźes cig kyang[1] gnang źu/

Inside white silk a promise came
For the bright moon's third night.
Please give to me one more oath,
Like unto that for the fifteenth.

1. Das: yang

40

ས་བཅུའི་དབྱིངས་སུ་བཞུགས་པའི།
དམ་ཅན་རྡོ་རྗེ་ཆོས་སྐྱོང་།
མཐུ་དང་ནུས་པ་ཡོད་ན།
བསྟན་པའི་དགྲ་བོ་སྒྲལ་དང་།

sa bcu'i dbyings su bźugs qa'i /
dam can rdo rje chos skyong/
mthu dang nus pa yod na/
bstan pa'i dgra bo sgral dang/

One with magical power
As Dam Chen Dorjay*
In the perfect sphere,**
May destroy Dharma foes.

*Tibetan : Dam can rdo rje (legs pa) is a well known Tantric deity of the class of the Drag bśed. I refer those interested to Helmut Hoffmann, *Symbolik der tibetischen Religionen und des Schamanismus,* (Stuttgart, 1967), p. 32.

**Literally the region of the ten steps of perfection, Tibetan : sa bcu'i dbyings; Sanscrit : daśabhūmidhātu.

41

ཁུ་བྱུག་མོན་ནས་འོངས་པས།
གནམ་ལོའི་ས་བཅུད་འཕེལ་སོང་།
ང་དང་བྱམས་པ་ཕྲད་ནས།
ལུས་སེམས་ལྷོད་པོར་ལངས་སོང་།

khu byug mon nas 'ongs pas[1]/
gnam lo'i sa bcud 'phel song/
nga dang byams ya phrad nas/
lus sems lhod por langs[2]song/

The cuckoo does come from Mon.*
The yearly rains do now fall.
I have encountered love.
I rest well content.

1. Das: pa'i
2. Das: lang

*Mon is a collection of Tibeto-Burmese speaking regions on the southern slopes of the Himalayas from Almora district west of Nepal to the Assam hills.

42

ཁྱི་དེ་སྟག་ཁྱི་གཟིག་ཁྱི།
མདའ་ཁ་སྟེར་ནས་འདྲིས་སོང་།
ནང་གི་སྟག་མོ་རས་འཇོམས།
འདྲིས་ནས་མཐུ་རུ་ལང་སོང་།

khyi de stag khyi[1] gzig khyi/
mda' kha ster nas 'dris song/
nang gi stag mo ras 'joms[2]/
'dris nas mthur[3] du[4] lang song/

The dog, tiger-dog, leopard-dog
Goes tame, when freshly fed;
The hairy tigress inside
Joined me, stood up, and roared!

1. Das: —
2. Das: 'dzoms
3. Das: mthu
4. Das: ru

43

ཤ་འཇམ་ལུས་པོ་འདྲིས་ཀྱང་།
བྱམས་པའི་གདེང་ཚོད་མི་ལོན།
ས་ལ་རི་མོ་བྲིས་པས།
ནམ་མཁའི་སྐར་ཚོད་ཐིག་འབྱུང་།

śa 'jam lus po 'dris kyang/
byams pa'i gdeng[1] tshod mi lon/
sa la ri mo bris pas[2]
nam mkha'i skar tshod thig 'byung/

I know her soft body,
But not of her love.
I draw figures on the sand,
And measure the distance to the sky.

1. Das: lting
2. Das: pa'i

44

ང་དང་བྱམས་པའི་སྡེབས་ས།
ལྷོ་རོང་ལྗོན་པའི་ནགས་གསེབ།
སྨྲ་མཁན་ནེ་ཙོ་མ་གཏོགས།
སུ་དང་གང་གིས་མི་ཤེས།

nga dang byams pa'i sdebs sa/
lho[1] rong ljon pa'i nags gseb[2]/
smra mkhan ne tso ma gtogs/
su dang gang gis mi[3] śes/

In the enchanting forest of
A southern valley, our love
Does meet. Save the talking
Parrot, no one else knows.

1. Das: lho'i
2. Das: bseb
3. Das: ma

45

སྨྲ་མཁན་ནེ་ཙོ་ཨོ་ཤེས།
གསང་ཁ་སྟོན་པ་མ་གནང་།
ལྷ་ས་མི་རྫོགས་མཐུག་ལ།
ཆུང་རྒྱལ་མི་སྤུས་དག་པ།

smra mkhan ne tso o śes/
gsang kha ston pa ma gnang/
lha sa mi rdzogs[1] mthug la/
chung rgyal mi spus dag pa/

The talking parrot does know
This teaching not to let go:
Lhasa has large numbers;
Chungjay* has pure beauties.

1. read: 'dzogs

*Tibetan : Chung rgyal, the name of a small settlement near the Potala where the Dalai Lama lives.

46

ང་ལ་ཡོད་པའི་ཆུང་འདྲིས།
ཆུང་རྒྱལ་གཞུང་ན་ཡོད་དོ།
ཁྱི་རྒན་རྒྱའུ་ཟེར་བ།
རྣམ་ཤེས་མི་ལས་ཙང་བ།

nga la yod[1] pa'i chung 'dris/
chung rgyal gźung na yod do/
khyi rgan rgya'u zer ba/
rnam śes mi las cang ba[2]/

I have a friend.
She lives in the conter of Chungjay.
Her name is Khyigen jay-u,*
I must keep this from the wise men.

1. Das: yongs
2. Das: ba'i; read: 'chang ba

*Tibetan : Khyi rgan rgya'u

47

སྲོད་ལ་ལངས་སོང་མ་ཟེར།

ཐོ་རེངས་ལོག་བྱུང་མ་ཟེར།

སྲོད་ལ་བྱམས་པ་བཙལ་བའི།

ཁ་བ་མང་པོ་བབ་བྱུང་།

srod la langs[1] song ma zer/
tho rengs[2] log byung ma zer/
srod la byams pa btsal ba'i/
kha ba mang po bab[3] byung/

Do not say :
'To leave at dusk and return at dawn'.
There will fall many snows
On those seeking love at dusk.

1. Das: lang
2. Das: rangs
3. Das : 'bab

48

པོ་ཏ་ལ་རུ་བཞུགས་དུས།
རིག་འཛིན་ཚངས་དབྱངས་རྒྱ་མཚོ།
ལྷ་ས་ཞོལ་དུ་སྡོད་དུས།
འཆལ་པོ་དང་བཟང་དབང་པོ།

po ta la ru bźugs dus/
rig 'dzin tsangs dbyangs rgya mtsho/
lha sa źol du sdod dus/
'chal[1] po dang bzang dbang po/

When at the Potala,
I am called Rinchen Tsangyang Gyatso;*
When in Lhasa and Shol,**
I am called Chepo and Zang wang po.***

1. Das: 'chel

*Tibetan : Rig 'dzin tshangs dbyangs rgya mtsho (- The learned ocean of pure song).

**Tibetan : Źol, the houses in this village, as well as Lhasa are generally whitewashed. The few that are painted yellow are held by tradition to be those that belonged to courtesans whom the Sixth Dalai Lama visited frequently. Shakabpa, loc. cit., p. 131.

***Tibetan : 'Chal po dang bzang dbang po (The fornicator and the powerful handsome one).

49

གསང་དང་མ་གསང་མི་འདུག།
ཞབས་རྗེས་གངས་ལ་བཞག་ནི།
ཤ་འཇམ་མལ་ས་ནང་གི།
སྙིང་ཐུབ་དུང་སེམས་ཅན་མ།

gsang dang ma gsang mi 'dug/
źabs rjes gangs la bźag gi[1]/
śa 'jam mal sa nang gi/
snying thub dung sems can ma/

I left foot prints in the snow;
No more secrets and non-secrets.
In the bedroom of my love,
Conch-white heart, body so tender.

1. Das: ni

50

ཨོ་ལོས་དགེ་ནོར་འཕྲོགས་པའི།
གཡོ་སྒྱུ་བཤད་པ་མིན་འགྲོ།
དབུ་ཞ་དབུ་ལ་བཞེས་སོང་།
དབུ་ལྕང་རྒྱབ་ལ་དབྱུགས་སོང་།

o los dge nor 'phrogs pa'i
g-yo sgyu bśad pa min 'gro/
dbu źva dbu la bźes song/
dbu lcang rgyab la dbyugs song/

This lad so slyly does steal
A wealth of true virtue,
A cap he wears on top,
Pigtail swings down the back.

51

ག་ལེར་ཕེབས་ཤིག་བྱས་པས།
ག་ལེར་བཞུགས་ཤིག་གསུང་གི།
ཐུགས་སེམས་སྐྱོ་ཡོང་བྱས་པས།
མགྱོགས་པོ་འཕྲད་ཡོང་གསུངས་བྱུང་།

ga ler[1] phebs śig[2] byas bas[3]/
ga ler[4] bźugs śig[5] gsung gi/
thugs sems skyo yong byas pas[6]
mgyogs po 'phrad yong gsungs byung/

I said goodbye to her.
She replied : "Goodbye".
Because this made her cry,
I said : "Soon again we say hi !"

1. Das: le
2. Das: cig
3. Das: pa'i
4. Das: le
5. Das: cig
6. Das: pa'i

52

བྱ་དེ་ཁྲུང་ཁྲུང་དཀར་མོ།
ང་ལ་གཤོག་རྩལ་གཡར་དང་།
ཐག་རིང་རྒྱང་ལ་མི་འགྲོ།
ལི་ཐང་བསྐོར་ནས་སླེབས་ཡོང་།

bya de khrung khrung dkar mo/
nga la gśog rtsal g-yar dang/
thag ring rgyang[1] la mi 'gro/
li thang bskor nas slebs yong/

If only white cranes
Do grant me wings,
I shall not go far;
Only to Lithang, then home.

1. Das: 'gyangs

53

ཤི་དེ་དམྱལ་བའི་ཡུལ་གྱི།
ཆོས་རྒྱལ་ལས་ཀྱི་མེ་ལོང་།
འདི་ན་ཁྲིག་ཁྲིག་མི་འདུག།
དེ་ནས་ཁྲིག་ཁྲིག་གནང་ཞུ།

śi de dmyal ba'i yul gyi/
chos rgyal las kyi me long/
'di khrig khrig mi 'dug/
de nas khrig khrig gnang źu/

At death, the mirror of deeds
Is held by Yama, the judge.
Here there is no justice.
There, please grant this justice.